I0818356

THIS JOURNAL

Belongs to

____

CLEAR MIND

A 5-Minute Journal

GAIN CLARITY AND GET THINGS DONE

INSIGHT STUDIO

SAN RAFAEL • LOS ANGELES • LONDON

Your time is your most valuable resource. In a world that tugs at your attention from a million different directions, it's more important than ever to pause and redefine your path.

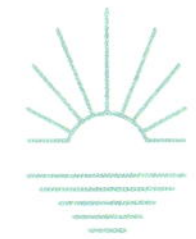

Why Brain Dumping Works

THE RESEARCH BEHIND THE METHOD

Our minds are overloaded. On any given day, we process over six thousand individual thoughts.[1] That mental traffic jam can leave us feeling anxious, distracted, and perpetually behind. That's where a daily brain-dump practice comes in.

A brain-dump is exactly what it sounds like—taking everything swirling around in your head and putting it onto paper. No judgment, no editing, no need to make it pretty. It's simply a tool to off-load your mind's clutter so you can see what's actually taking up space.

Research supports this practice. Studies show that writing about our thoughts and worries can reduce intrusive rumination by up to 30%, freeing up mental energy for more meaningful focus.[2,3] Expressive writing is also linked to lower stress, better mood regulation, and even improved working memory.[4,5] In short, getting thoughts out of your head makes room for what matters most.

But brain dumping isn't just about stress relief; it's about gaining clarity and prioritizing your time and energy.

When you see your thoughts laid out on the page, patterns emerge. Priorities begin to reveal themselves before your eyes, and pressures that felt overwhelming before start to shrink. This simple habit can help you organize your to-dos, process tricky emotions, and create a road map for moving forward.

In fact, a study from the University of Tokyo found that people who regularly wrote down their thoughts before beginning tasks experienced improved cognitive performance and faster decision-making.[2] Why? Because the brain can only hold so much at one time. Cognitive load theory suggests that when we try to mentally juggle too many things at once, we become less efficient, more forgetful, and emotionally drained.[6] Writing things down literally frees up working memory.

Even just five to ten minutes of unstructured writing have been shown to lower cortisol (the stress hormone) and calm the nervous system.[5] That's why brain dumping isn't just a productivity hack; it's a wellness habit.

Let this journal be your safe space to untangle the mental mess. There's no right or wrong way to use it. Just show up, be honest, and give your mind a chance to breathe.

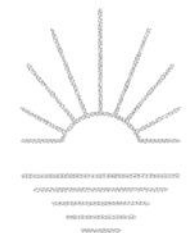

Getting Started: How to Use This Journal

YOUR JOURNEY TO A CLEARER MIND

DAILY BRAIN DUMP PAGES

Start your day on the left-hand page. This is the dedicated brain-dump space where you'll unload everything on your mind—from worries and reminders to creative ideas and nagging to dos. Don't overthink it. Simply let your thoughts spill out freely. This process alone helps reduce mental noise, organize your thinking, and lower stress.

The right-hand page provides space to focus your day with intention. At the top, list your three main priorities for the day. To the right, you'll find space to map out three action steps to accomplish them. This breaks big goals into manageable pieces, reduces feeling overwhelmed, and helps you maintain momentum. Be as specific as possible. Instead of "work on presentation," try "outline key points for slides 1–5." This makes it easier to start and finish tasks.

The bottom left column provides a section for you to note what you can delegate, press pause on, or let go of today. We often overload ourselves out of habit. Use this area to remind yourself it's okay to hand off tasks, delay nonurgent items, and release expectations that aren't serving you. This is a powerful way to lighten your load and prioritize your well-being.

Use the bottom-right quadrant of the page for any open notes. This is the place to reflect on how you felt, what your biggest wins and challenges were, and anything meaningful you learned. It's also a great spot to jot down intentions for tomorrow.

WEEKLY PRIORITY PAGES

At the close of each week, you'll find a dedicated spread designed to help you step back, sort your thoughts, and bring order to what matters most. The right-hand page is divided into four open sections that you can use in whichever way feels most helpful. Here are a few proven approaches you might try:

The Eisenhower Matrix

Popularized by President Dwight D. Eisenhower, this system groups tasks into four boxes: important and urgent, important but less urgent, urgent but less important, and neither important nor urgent. Once laid out, the top-left tasks deserve immediate attention, the top-right tasks should be scheduled, the bottom-left can often be delegated, and the bottom-right are best to be released entirely.

By Timeline

Instead of urgency, you might want to focus on when you'll handle things. A simple system is: "Now, Next, Later, Never." Place each task where it fits, and let the list guide your action steps.

By Category

If your weekly brain dumps show recurring areas of life, you can group them into four themes. For instance: "Family, Work, Home, Health" or, for special projects or travel, "Packing, Booking, Planning, Details."

By Nature of Task

Sometimes it helps to sort based on what kind of effort the task requires. For example: "To Do, To Research, To Communicate, and To Resolve."

There's no perfect way to use this journal. Some days you'll fill every section; other days, just getting your thoughts on paper might be enough. The goal is to build a habit that helps you feel clear, focused, a little more at peace, and ready to tackle all the challenges that come your way.

THE EISENHOWER MATRIX

Important & Urgent	*Important & Less Urgent*
Urgent & Less Important	*Less Important & Less Urgent*

BY TIMELINE

Now	*Next*
Later	*Never*

BY CATEGORY

Family	*Work*
Home	*Health*

BY NATURE OF TASK

To Do	*To Research*
To Communicate	*To Resolve*

"Clarity about what matters provides clarity about what does not."

– Greg McKeown, *Essentialism*

Brain Dump Pages

CLEAR YOUR MIND AND GET THINGS DONE

____ / ____ /20____

Brain Dump:

Top three priorities for today:

1

2

3

Three action steps to accomplish each priority:

☐

☐

☐

☐

☐

☐

☐

☐

☐

Tasks to delegate, schedule, or let go of:

Notes:

___/___/20___

Brain Dump:

Top three priorities for today:

1

2

3

Three action steps to accomplish each priority:

- [ ]
- [ ]
- [ ]

- [ ]
- [ ]
- [ ]

- [ ]
- [ ]
- [ ]

Tasks to delegate, schedule, or let go of:

Notes:

____/____/20____

Brain Dump:

Top three priorities for today:

1

2

3

Three action steps to accomplish each priority:

- ☐
- ☐
- ☐

- ☐
- ☐
- ☐

- ☐
- ☐
- ☐

Tasks to delegate, schedule, or let go of:

Notes:

____/____/20____

Brain Dump:

Top three priorities for today:

1

2

3

Three action steps to accomplish each priority:

☐

☐

☐

☐

☐

☐

☐

☐

☐

Tasks to delegate, schedule, or let go of:

Notes:

____/____/20____

Brain Dump:

Top three priorities for today:

1 ______

______

______

2 ______

______

______

3 ______

______

______

Three action steps to accomplish each priority:

- ☐ ______
- ☐ ______
- ☐ ______

- ☐ ______
- ☐ ______
- ☐ ______

- ☐ ______
- ☐ ______
- ☐ ______

Tasks to delegate, schedule, or let go of:

Notes:

____/____/20____

Brain Dump:

Top three priorities for today:

Three action steps to accomplish each priority:

1

- [ ]
- [ ]
- [ ]

2

- [ ]
- [ ]
- [ ]

3

- [ ]
- [ ]
- [ ]

Tasks to delegate, schedule, or let go of:

Notes:

___/___/20___

Brain Dump:

Top three priorities for today:

1 ______

______

______

2 ______

______

______

3 ______

______

______

Three action steps to accomplish each priority:

☐ ______

☐ ______

☐ ______

☐ ______

☐ ______

☐ ______

☐ ______

☐ ______

☐ ______

Tasks to delegate, schedule, or let go of:

Notes:

"A clear mind sees simple truths: what to hold close, what to release, and where to go next."

– Stoic and essentialist philosophy

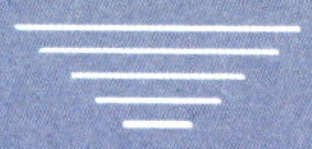

Planning for the Week of:

____/________/20____

___/___/20___

Brain Dump:

Top three priorities for today:

1 ______________________________

2 ______________________________

3 ______________________________

Three action steps to accomplish each priority:

- [ ]
- [ ]
- [ ]

- [ ]
- [ ]
- [ ]

- [ ]
- [ ]
- [ ]

Tasks to delegate, schedule, or let go of:

Notes:

___/___/20___

Brain Dump:

Top three priorities for today:

1

2

3

Three action steps to accomplish each priority:

☐

☐

☐

☐

☐

☐

☐

☐

☐

Tasks to delegate, schedule, or let go of:

Notes:

____ / ____ /20____

Brain Dump:

Top three priorities for today:

1 ____________________

2 ____________________

3 ____________________

Three action steps to accomplish each priority:

- ☐
- ☐
- ☐
- ☐
- ☐
- ☐
- ☐
- ☐
- ☐

Tasks to delegate, schedule, or let go of:

Notes:

___/___/20___

Brain Dump:

Top three priorities for today:

1 ____________________

2 ____________________

3 ____________________

Three action steps to accomplish each priority:

- ☐
- ☐
- ☐
- ☐
- ☐
- ☐
- ☐
- ☐
- ☐

Tasks to delegate, schedule, or let go of:

Notes:

____/____/20____

Brain Dump:

Top three priorities for today:

1 ______________________

____

____

2 ______________________

____

____

3 ______________________

____

____

Three action steps to accomplish each priority:

- [ ] ______________________
- [ ] ______________________
- [ ] ______________________

- [ ] ______________________
- [ ] ______________________
- [ ] ______________________

- [ ] ______________________
- [ ] ______________________
- [ ] ______________________

Tasks to delegate, schedule, or let go of:

Notes:

___/___/20___

Brain Dump:

Top three priorities for today:

1 __________

2 __________

3 __________

Three action steps to accomplish each priority:

☐ __________
☐ __________
☐ __________

☐ __________
☐ __________
☐ __________

☐ __________
☐ __________
☐ __________

Tasks to delegate, schedule, or let go of:

Notes:

____/____/20____

Brain Dump:

Top three priorities for today:

1 __________

2 __________

3 __________

Three action steps to accomplish each priority:

- ☐
- ☐
- ☐
- ☐
- ☐
- ☐
- ☐
- ☐
- ☐

Tasks to delegate, schedule, or let go of:

Notes:

"The nearer a man comes to a calm mind, the closer he is to strength."

– Marcus Aurelius

Planning for the Week of:

____/________/20____

____/____/20____

Brain Dump:

Top three priorities for today:

1 ________________________

2 ________________________

3 ________________________

Three action steps to accomplish each priority:

- [ ]
- [ ]
- [ ]

- [ ]
- [ ]
- [ ]

- [ ]
- [ ]
- [ ]

Tasks to delegate, schedule, or let go of:

Notes:

___/___/20___

Brain Dump:

Top three priorities for today:

1 ____________________

2 ____________________

3 ____________________

Three action steps to accomplish each priority:

- ☐
- ☐
- ☐

- ☐
- ☐
- ☐

- ☐
- ☐
- ☐

Tasks to delegate, schedule, or let go of:

Notes:

____ /____ /20____

Brain Dump:

Top three priorities for today:

1 __________

____

____

2 __________

____

____

3 __________

____

____

Three action steps to accomplish each priority:

- ☐ __________
- ☐ __________
- ☐ __________

- ☐ __________
- ☐ __________
- ☐ __________

- ☐ __________
- ☐ __________
- ☐ __________

Tasks to delegate, schedule, or let go of:

Notes:

___/___/20___

Brain Dump:

Top three priorities for today:

1

2

3

Three action steps to accomplish each priority:

- [ ]
- [ ]
- [ ]
- [ ]
- [ ]
- [ ]
- [ ]
- [ ]
- [ ]

Tasks to delegate, schedule, or let go of:

Notes:

___/___/20___

Brain Dump:

Top three priorities for today:

1 ______________________________

____

____

2 ______________________________

____

____

3 ______________________________

____

____

Three action steps to accomplish each priority:

☐ ______________________________

☐ ______________________________

☐ ______________________________

☐ ______________________________

☐ ______________________________

☐ ______________________________

☐ ______________________________

☐ ______________________________

☐ ______________________________

Tasks to delegate, schedule, or let go of:

____

____

____

____

____

____

____

____

____

____

Notes:

____

____

____

____

____

____

____

____

____

____

____

____

____/____/20____

Brain Dump:

Top three priorities for today:

1

2

3

Three action steps to accomplish each priority:

☐

☐

☐

☐

☐

☐

☐

☐

☐

Tasks to delegate, schedule, or let go of:

Notes:

____/____ /20____

Brain Dump:

Top three priorities for today:

1 __________

2 __________

3 __________

Three action steps to accomplish each priority:

- [ ]
- [ ]
- [ ]

- [ ]
- [ ]
- [ ]

- [ ]
- [ ]
- [ ]

Tasks to delegate, schedule, or let go of:

Notes:

"The mind is everything; what you think, you become."

– Unknown

Planning for the Week of:

____/________/20____

___/___/20___

Brain Dump:

Top three priorities for today:

1 __________

2 __________

3 __________

Three action steps to accomplish each priority:

- [ ]
- [ ]
- [ ]

- [ ]
- [ ]
- [ ]

- [ ]
- [ ]
- [ ]

Tasks to delegate, schedule, or let go of:

Notes:

___/___/20___

Brain Dump:

Top three priorities for today:

1 ______

______

______

2 ______

______

______

3 ______

______

______

Three action steps to accomplish each priority:

☐ ______

☐ ______

☐ ______

☐ ______

☐ ______

☐ ______

☐ ______

☐ ______

☐ ______

Tasks to delegate, schedule, or let go of:

Notes:

____/____/20____

Brain Dump:

Top three priorities for today:

1

2

3

Three action steps to accomplish each priority:

- [ ]
- [ ]
- [ ]

- [ ]
- [ ]
- [ ]

- [ ]
- [ ]
- [ ]

Tasks to delegate, schedule, or let go of:

Notes:

____/____/20____

Brain Dump:

Top three priorities for today:

1 ______________________

____

____

2 ______________________

____

____

3 ______________________

____

____

Three action steps to accomplish each priority:

☐ ______________________

☐ ______________________

☐ ______________________

☐ ______________________

☐ ______________________

☐ ______________________

☐ ______________________

☐ ______________________

☐ ______________________

Tasks to delegate, schedule, or let go of:

Notes:

___/___/20___

Brain Dump:

Top three priorities for today:

1 __________

____

____

2 __________

____

____

3 __________

____

____

Three action steps to accomplish each priority:

- ☐ __________
- ☐ __________
- ☐ __________

- ☐ __________
- ☐ __________
- ☐ __________

- ☐ __________
- ☐ __________
- ☐ __________

Tasks to delegate, schedule, or let go of:

Notes:

___/___/20___

Brain Dump:

Top three priorities for today:

1

2

3

Three action steps to accomplish each priority:

- [ ]
- [ ]
- [ ]

- [ ]
- [ ]
- [ ]

- [ ]
- [ ]
- [ ]

Tasks to delegate, schedule, or let go of:

Notes:

____ / ____ /20____

Brain Dump:

Top three priorities for today:

1 ______

______

______

2 ______

______

______

3 ______

______

______

Three action steps to accomplish each priority:

- [ ] ______
- [ ] ______
- [ ] ______

- [ ] ______
- [ ] ______
- [ ] ______

- [ ] ______
- [ ] ______
- [ ] ______

Tasks to delegate, schedule, or let go of:

Notes:

"Concentrate all your thoughts upon the work at hand. The sun's rays do not burn until brought to a focus."

– Alexander Graham Bell

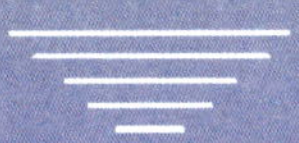

Planning for the Week of:

____/________/20____

____/____/20____

Brain Dump:

Top three priorities for today:

1 ____________________

2 ____________________

3 ____________________

Three action steps to accomplish each priority:

☐
☐
☐

☐
☐
☐

☐
☐
☐

Tasks to delegate, schedule, or let go of:

Notes:

____/____/20____

Brain Dump:

Top three priorities for today:

1 ____________________

2 ____________________

3 ____________________

Three action steps to accomplish each priority:

- ☐
- ☐
- ☐

- ☐
- ☐
- ☐

- ☐
- ☐
- ☐

Tasks to delegate, schedule, or let go of:

Notes:

____/____/20____

Brain Dump:

Top three priorities for today:

1

2

3

Three action steps to accomplish each priority:

- [ ]
- [ ]
- [ ]

- [ ]
- [ ]
- [ ]

- [ ]
- [ ]
- [ ]

Tasks to delegate, schedule, or let go of:

Notes:

____/____/20____

Brain Dump:

Top three priorities for today:

1 ____________________

2 ____________________

3 ____________________

Three action steps to accomplish each priority:

- [ ]
- [ ]
- [ ]

- [ ]
- [ ]
- [ ]

- [ ]
- [ ]
- [ ]

Tasks to delegate, schedule, or let go of:

Notes:

____ / ____ /20____

Brain Dump:

Top three priorities for today:

1 ____________________

2 ____________________

3 ____________________

Three action steps to accomplish each priority:

- ☐
- ☐
- ☐

- ☐
- ☐
- ☐

- ☐
- ☐
- ☐

Tasks to delegate, schedule, or let go of:

Notes:

___/___/20___

Brain Dump:

Top three priorities for today:

1 ____________________

2 ____________________

3 ____________________

Three action steps to accomplish each priority:

- ☐
- ☐
- ☐

- ☐
- ☐
- ☐

- ☐
- ☐
- ☐

Tasks to delegate, schedule, or let go of:

Notes:

____/____/20____

Brain Dump:

Top three priorities for today:

1 __________

2 __________

3 __________

Three action steps to accomplish each priority:

☐

☐

☐

☐

☐

☐

☐

☐

☐

Tasks to delegate, schedule, or let go of:

Notes:

“He who is everywhere is nowhere.”

– Seneca

Planning for the Week of:

____/_______/20____

____/____/20____

Brain Dump:

Top three priorities for today:

1 ______________________

____

____

2 ______________________

____

____

3 ______________________

____

____

Three action steps to accomplish each priority:

☐ ______________________

☐ ______________________

☐ ______________________

☐ ______________________

☐ ______________________

☐ ______________________

☐ ______________________

☐ ______________________

☐ ______________________

Tasks to delegate, schedule, or let go of:

____

____

____

____

____

____

____

____

____

____

Notes:

____

____

____

____

____

____

____

____

____

____

____

____

____/____/20____

Brain Dump:

Top three priorities for today:

1 ______

______

______

2 ______

______

______

3 ______

______

______

Three action steps to accomplish each priority:

- ☐ ______
- ☐ ______
- ☐ ______

- ☐ ______
- ☐ ______
- ☐ ______

- ☐ ______
- ☐ ______
- ☐ ______

Tasks to delegate, schedule, or let go of:

Notes:

____/____/20____

Brain Dump:

Top three priorities for today:

1 ____________________

2 ____________________

3 ____________________

Three action steps to accomplish each priority:

☐

☐

☐

☐

☐

☐

☐

☐

☐

Tasks to delegate, schedule, or let go of:

Notes:

____/____/20____

Brain Dump:

Top three priorities for today:

1 ______

______

______

2 ______

______

______

3 ______

______

______

Three action steps to accomplish each priority:

- [ ] ______
- [ ] ______
- [ ] ______

- [ ] ______
- [ ] ______
- [ ] ______

- [ ] ______
- [ ] ______
- [ ] ______

Tasks to delegate, schedule, or let go of:

Notes:

___/___/20___

Brain Dump:

Top three priorities for today:

1

2

3

Three action steps to accomplish each priority:

- [ ]
- [ ]
- [ ]
- [ ]
- [ ]
- [ ]
- [ ]
- [ ]
- [ ]

Tasks to delegate, schedule, or let go of:

Notes:

____ / ____ /20____

Brain Dump:

Top three priorities for today:

1 ______________________

____

____

2 ______________________

____

____

3 ______________________

____

____

Three action steps to accomplish each priority:

- [ ] ______________________
- [ ] ______________________
- [ ] ______________________

- [ ] ______________________
- [ ] ______________________
- [ ] ______________________

- [ ] ______________________
- [ ] ______________________
- [ ] ______________________

Tasks to delegate, schedule, or let go of:

Notes:

____/____/20____

Brain Dump:

Top three priorities for today:

1 ________________

____

____

2 ________________

____

____

3 ________________

____

____

Three action steps to accomplish each priority:

- ☐ ________________
- ☐ ________________
- ☐ ________________

- ☐ ________________
- ☐ ________________
- ☐ ________________

- ☐ ________________
- ☐ ________________
- ☐ ________________

Tasks to delegate, schedule, or let go of:

Notes:

"Nothing is so conducive to greatness of mind as the ability to examine calmly and without haste everything that happens in life."

– Marcus Aurelius

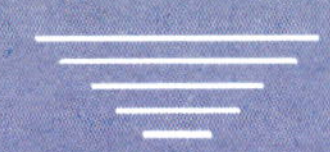

Planning for the Week of:

____/________/20____

___/___/20___

Brain Dump:

Top three priorities for today:

1 ______

______

______

2 ______

______

______

3 ______

______

______

Three action steps to accomplish each priority:

- [ ] ______
- [ ] ______
- [ ] ______

- [ ] ______
- [ ] ______
- [ ] ______

- [ ] ______
- [ ] ______
- [ ] ______

Tasks to delegate, schedule, or let go of:

Notes:

___/___/20___

Brain Dump:

Top three priorities for today:

1 ____________________

____

____

2 ____________________

____

____

3 ____________________

____

____

Three action steps to accomplish each priority:

- ☐ ____________________
- ☐ ____________________
- ☐ ____________________

- ☐ ____________________
- ☐ ____________________
- ☐ ____________________

- ☐ ____________________
- ☐ ____________________
- ☐ ____________________

Tasks to delegate, schedule, or let go of:

Notes:

___/___/20___

Brain Dump:

Top three priorities for today:

1 ____________________

2 ____________________

3 ____________________

Three action steps to accomplish each priority:

- [ ]
- [ ]
- [ ]

- [ ]
- [ ]
- [ ]

- [ ]
- [ ]
- [ ]

Tasks to delegate, schedule, or let go of:

Notes:

___/___/20___

Brain Dump:

Top three priorities for today:

1

2

3

Three action steps to accomplish each priority:

- [ ]
- [ ]
- [ ]

- [ ]
- [ ]
- [ ]

- [ ]
- [ ]
- [ ]

Tasks to delegate, schedule, or let go of:

Notes:

____/____/20____

Brain Dump:

Top three priorities for today:

1 ___

2 ___

3 ___

Three action steps to accomplish each priority:

- ☐
- ☐
- ☐
- ☐
- ☐
- ☐
- ☐
- ☐
- ☐

Tasks to delegate, schedule, or let go of:

Notes:

____/____/20____

Brain Dump:

Top three priorities for today:

1

2

3

Three action steps to accomplish each priority:

- [ ]
- [ ]
- [ ]

- [ ]
- [ ]
- [ ]

- [ ]
- [ ]
- [ ]

Tasks to delegate, schedule, or let go of:

Notes:

____ /____ /20____

Brain Dump:

Top three priorities for today:

1

2

3

Three action steps to accomplish each priority:

☐
☐
☐

☐
☐
☐

☐
☐
☐

Tasks to delegate, schedule, or let go of:

Notes:

"If you chase two rabbits, you will not catch either one."

– Chinese proverb

Planning for the Week of:

___/______/20___

____/____/20____

Brain Dump:

Top three priorities for today:

1 ____________________

2 ____________________

3 ____________________

Three action steps to accomplish each priority:

- ☐
- ☐
- ☐
- ☐
- ☐
- ☐
- ☐
- ☐
- ☐

Tasks to delegate, schedule, or let go of:

Notes:

___/___/20___

Brain Dump:

Top three priorities for today:

1 ____________________

2 ____________________

3 ____________________

Three action steps to accomplish each priority:

- ☐
- ☐
- ☐

- ☐
- ☐
- ☐

- ☐
- ☐
- ☐

Tasks to delegate, schedule, or let go of:

Notes:

____/____/20____

Brain Dump:

Top three priorities for today:

1 ____________________

____

____

2 ____________________

____

____

3 ____________________

____

____

Three action steps to accomplish each priority:

- ☐ ____________________
- ☐ ____________________
- ☐ ____________________

- ☐ ____________________
- ☐ ____________________
- ☐ ____________________

- ☐ ____________________
- ☐ ____________________
- ☐ ____________________

Tasks to delegate, schedule, or let go of:

Notes:

___/___/20___

Brain Dump:

Top three priorities for today:

1 ____________________

2 ____________________

3 ____________________

Three action steps to accomplish each priority:

- ☐
- ☐
- ☐
- ☐
- ☐
- ☐
- ☐
- ☐
- ☐

Tasks to delegate, schedule, or let go of:

Notes:

____/____/20____

Brain Dump:

Top three priorities for today:

1 ______________________________

____

____

2 ______________________________

____

____

3 ______________________________

____

____

Three action steps to accomplish each priority:

☐ ______________________________

☐ ______________________________

☐ ______________________________

☐ ______________________________

☐ ______________________________

☐ ______________________________

☐ ______________________________

☐ ______________________________

☐ ______________________________

Tasks to delegate, schedule, or let go of:

____

____

____

____

____

____

____

____

____

____

Notes:

____

____

____

____

____

____

____

____

____

____

____

____

____/____/20____

Brain Dump:

Top three priorities for today:

1 ______

______

______

2 ______

______

______

3 ______

______

______

Three action steps to accomplish each priority:

- ☐ ______
- ☐ ______
- ☐ ______

- ☐ ______
- ☐ ______
- ☐ ______

- ☐ ______
- ☐ ______
- ☐ ______

Tasks to delegate, schedule, or let go of:

Notes:

____ / ____ /20____

Brain Dump:

Top three priorities for today:

1 ______

______

______

2 ______

______

______

3 ______

______

______

Three action steps to accomplish each priority:

- [ ] ______
- [ ] ______
- [ ] ______

- [ ] ______
- [ ] ______
- [ ] ______

- [ ] ______
- [ ] ______
- [ ] ______

Tasks to delegate, schedule, or let go of:

Notes:

"Our life is frittered away by detail . . . Simplify, simplify."

– Henry David Thoreau

Planning for the Week of:

____/________/20____

___/___/20___

Brain Dump:

Top three priorities for today:

1 __________

____

____

2 __________

____

____

3 __________

____

____

Three action steps to accomplish each priority:

- ☐ __________
- ☐ __________
- ☐ __________

- ☐ __________
- ☐ __________
- ☐ __________

- ☐ __________
- ☐ __________
- ☐ __________

Tasks to delegate, schedule, or let go of:

Notes:

___/___/20___

Brain Dump:

Top three priorities for today:

1 ____________________

____

____

2 ____________________

____

____

3 ____________________

____

____

Three action steps to accomplish each priority:

- [ ] ____________________
- [ ] ____________________
- [ ] ____________________

- [ ] ____________________
- [ ] ____________________
- [ ] ____________________

- [ ] ____________________
- [ ] ____________________
- [ ] ____________________

Tasks to delegate, schedule, or let go of:

Notes:

___/___/20___

Brain Dump:

Top three priorities for today:

1

2

3

Three action steps to accomplish each priority:

- ☐
- ☐
- ☐

- ☐
- ☐
- ☐

- ☐
- ☐
- ☐

Tasks to delegate, schedule, or let go of:

Notes:

____/____/20____

Brain Dump:

Top three priorities for today:

1 ____________________

2 ____________________

3 ____________________

Three action steps to accomplish each priority:

☐ ☐ ☐

☐ ☐ ☐

☐ ☐ ☐

Tasks to delegate, schedule, or let go of:

Notes:

____/____/20____

Brain Dump:

Top three priorities for today:

1 __________

____

____

2 __________

____

____

3 __________

____

____

Three action steps to accomplish each priority:

- ☐
- ☐
- ☐

- ☐
- ☐
- ☐

- ☐
- ☐
- ☐

Tasks to delegate, schedule, or let go of:

Notes:

___/___/20___

Brain Dump:

Top three priorities for today:

1 __________

2 __________

3 __________

Three action steps to accomplish each priority:

- ☐
- ☐
- ☐
- ☐
- ☐
- ☐
- ☐
- ☐
- ☐

Tasks to delegate, schedule, or let go of:

Notes:

____ /____ /20____

Brain Dump:

Top three priorities for today:

1 ______

______

______

2 ______

______

______

3 ______

______

______

Three action steps to accomplish each priority:

☐ ______

☐ ______

☐ ______

☐ ______

☐ ______

☐ ______

☐ ______

☐ ______

☐ ______

Tasks to delegate, schedule, or let go of:

Notes:

"It is not that we have a short time to live, but that we waste a lot of it."

– Seneca

Planning for the Week of:

____/________/20____

____/____/20____

Brain Dump:

Top three priorities for today:

1 ______

______

______

2 ______

______

______

3 ______

______

______

Three action steps to accomplish each priority:

- [ ] ______
- [ ] ______
- [ ] ______

- [ ] ______
- [ ] ______
- [ ] ______

- [ ] ______
- [ ] ______
- [ ] ______

Tasks to delegate, schedule, or let go of:

Notes:

____/____/20____

Brain Dump:

Top three priorities for today:

1 ____________________

2 ____________________

3 ____________________

Three action steps to accomplish each priority:

- ☐
- ☐
- ☐

- ☐
- ☐
- ☐

- ☐
- ☐
- ☐

Tasks to delegate, schedule, or let go of:

Notes:

____/____/20____

Brain Dump:

Top three priorities for today:

1 __________

2 __________

3 __________

Three action steps to accomplish each priority:

- ☐
- ☐
- ☐
- ☐
- ☐
- ☐
- ☐
- ☐
- ☐

Tasks to delegate, schedule, or let go of:

Notes:

___/___/20___

Brain Dump:

Top three priorities for today:

1 ____________________

2 ____________________

3 ____________________

Three action steps to accomplish each priority:

- ☐
- ☐
- ☐

- ☐
- ☐
- ☐

- ☐
- ☐
- ☐

Tasks to delegate, schedule, or let go of:

Notes:

____/____/20____

Brain Dump:

Top three priorities for today:

1 ____________________

2 ____________________

3 ____________________

Three action steps to accomplish each priority:

☐

☐

☐

☐

☐

☐

☐

☐

☐

Tasks to delegate, schedule, or let go of:

Notes:

____ / ____ /20____

Brain Dump:

Top three priorities for today:

1

2

3

Three action steps to accomplish each priority:

- [ ]
- [ ]
- [ ]
- [ ]
- [ ]
- [ ]
- [ ]
- [ ]
- [ ]

Tasks to delegate, schedule, or let go of:

Notes:

____ / ____ /20____

Brain Dump:

Top three priorities for today:

1 ______

______

______

2 ______

______

______

3 ______

______

______

Three action steps to accomplish each priority:

- ☐ ______
- ☐ ______
- ☐ ______

- ☐ ______
- ☐ ______
- ☐ ______

- ☐ ______
- ☐ ______
- ☐ ______

Tasks to delegate, schedule, or let go of:

Notes:

MOMENT OF INSPIRATION

“Time abides long enough for those who make use of it.”

– Leonardo da Vinci

Planning for the Week of:

____ / ________ /20____

___/___/20___

Brain Dump:

Top three priorities for today:

1 ______________________

____

____

2 ______________________

____

____

3 ______________________

____

____

Three action steps to accomplish each priority:

- ☐ ______________________
- ☐ ______________________
- ☐ ______________________

- ☐ ______________________
- ☐ ______________________
- ☐ ______________________

- ☐ ______________________
- ☐ ______________________
- ☐ ______________________

Tasks to delegate, schedule, or let go of:

Notes:

___/___/20___

Brain Dump:

Top three priorities for today:

1 ____________________

2 ____________________

3 ____________________

Three action steps to accomplish each priority:

☐

☐

☐

☐

☐

☐

☐

☐

☐

Tasks to delegate, schedule, or let go of:

Notes:

____/____/20____

Brain Dump:

Top three priorities for today:

1 ______________________

____

____

2 ______________________

____

____

3 ______________________

____

____

Three action steps to accomplish each priority:

☐ ______________________

☐ ______________________

☐ ______________________

☐ ______________________

☐ ______________________

☐ ______________________

☐ ______________________

☐ ______________________

☐ ______________________

Tasks to delegate, schedule, or let go of:

Notes:

____ / ____ /20____

Brain Dump:

Top three priorities for today:

1 ____________________

____

____

2 ____________________

____

____

3 ____________________

____

____

Three action steps to accomplish each priority:

☐ ____________________

☐ ____________________

☐ ____________________

☐ ____________________

☐ ____________________

☐ ____________________

☐ ____________________

☐ ____________________

☐ ____________________

Tasks to delegate, schedule, or let go of:

Notes:

____ / ____ /20____

Brain Dump:

Top three priorities for today:

1

2

3

Three action steps to accomplish each priority:

☐

☐

☐

☐

☐

☐

☐

☐

☐

Tasks to delegate, schedule, or let go of:

Notes:

____ / ____ /20____

Brain Dump:

Top three priorities for today:

1 ____________________

____

____

2 ____________________

____

____

3 ____________________

____

____

Three action steps to accomplish each priority:

☐ ____________________

☐ ____________________

☐ ____________________

☐ ____________________

☐ ____________________

☐ ____________________

☐ ____________________

☐ ____________________

☐ ____________________

Tasks to delegate, schedule, or let go of:

Notes:

___/___/20___

Brain Dump:

Top three priorities for today:

1 __________

____

____

2 __________

____

____

3 __________

____

____

Three action steps to accomplish each priority:

- ☐ __________
- ☐ __________
- ☐ __________

- ☐ __________
- ☐ __________
- ☐ __________

- ☐ __________
- ☐ __________
- ☐ __________

Tasks to delegate, schedule, or let go of:

Notes:

___/___/20___

Brain Dump:

Top three priorities for today:

1

2

3

Three action steps to accomplish each priority:

- [ ]
- [ ]
- [ ]
- [ ]
- [ ]
- [ ]
- [ ]
- [ ]
- [ ]

Tasks to delegate, schedule, or let go of:

Notes:

"The shorter way to do many things is to only do one thing at a time."

– Wolfgang Amadeus Mozart

Planning for the Week of:

____/________/20____

___/___/20___

Brain Dump:

Top three priorities for today:

1 ______________________________

____

____

2 ______________________________

____

____

3 ______________________________

____

____

Three action steps to accomplish each priority:

- [ ] ______________________________
- [ ] ______________________________
- [ ] ______________________________

- [ ] ______________________________
- [ ] ______________________________
- [ ] ______________________________

- [ ] ______________________________
- [ ] ______________________________
- [ ] ______________________________

Tasks to delegate, schedule, or let go of:

Notes:

____/____/20____

Brain Dump:

Top three priorities for today:

1 ____________________

____

____

2 ____________________

____

____

3 ____________________

____

____

Three action steps to accomplish each priority:

- ☐ ____________________
- ☐ ____________________
- ☐ ____________________

- ☐ ____________________
- ☐ ____________________
- ☐ ____________________

- ☐ ____________________
- ☐ ____________________
- ☐ ____________________

Tasks to delegate, schedule, or let go of:

Notes:

____ / ____ /20____

Brain Dump:

Top three priorities for today:

1 __________

2 __________

3 __________

Three action steps to accomplish each priority:

- ☐
- ☐
- ☐

- ☐
- ☐
- ☐

- ☐
- ☐
- ☐

Tasks to delegate, schedule, or let go of:

Notes:

___/___/20___

Brain Dump:

Top three priorities for today:

1

2

3

Three action steps to accomplish each priority:

- [ ]
- [ ]
- [ ]
- [ ]
- [ ]
- [ ]
- [ ]
- [ ]
- [ ]

Tasks to delegate, schedule, or let go of:

Notes:

____/____/20____

Brain Dump:

Top three priorities for today:

1

2

3

Three action steps to accomplish each priority:

- ☐
- ☐
- ☐

- ☐
- ☐
- ☐

- ☐
- ☐
- ☐

Tasks to delegate, schedule, or let go of:

Notes:

____/____/20____

Brain Dump:

Top three priorities for today:

1 ____________________

____

____

2 ____________________

____

____

3 ____________________

____

____

Three action steps to accomplish each priority:

☐ ____________________

☐ ____________________

☐ ____________________

☐ ____________________

☐ ____________________

☐ ____________________

☐ ____________________

☐ ____________________

☐ ____________________

Tasks to delegate, schedule, or let go of:

Notes:

___/___/20___

Brain Dump:

Top three priorities for today:

1 __________

____

____

2 __________

____

____

3 __________

____

____

Three action steps to accomplish each priority:

- ☐ __________
- ☐ __________
- ☐ __________

- ☐ __________
- ☐ __________
- ☐ __________

- ☐ __________
- ☐ __________
- ☐ __________

Tasks to delegate, schedule, or let go of:

Notes:

"What we hope ever to do with ease, we must first learn to do with diligence."

– Samuel Johnson

Planning for the Week of:

____/________/20____

____/____/20____

Notes:

"Begin, be bold, and venture to be wise."

– Horace

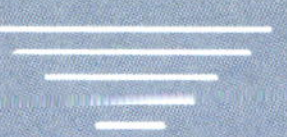

WORKS CITED

1. Meier, Matt L., et al. The Number of Thoughts Individuals Have per Day: Estimates from a Naturalistic Observation Study. *Nature Communications*, vol. 11, no. 1, 2020, article 2639.

2. Masicampo, E. J., and Roy F. Baumeister. Consider It Done! Plan Making Can Eliminate the Cognitive Effects of Unfulfilled Goals. *Journal of Personality and Social Psychology*, vol. 101, no. 4, 2011, pp. 667–683.

3. Baumeister, Roy F., et al. Bad Is Stronger than Good. *Review of General Psychology*, vol. 5, no. 4, 2001, pp. 323–370.

4. Pennebaker, James W. Writing About Emotional Experiences as a Therapeutic Process. *Psychological Science*, vol. 8, no. 3, 1997, pp. 162–166.

5. Smyth, Joshua M. Written Emotional Expression: Effect Sizes, Outcome Types, and Moderating Variables. *Journal of Consulting and Clinical Psychology*, vol. 66, no. 1, 1998, pp. 174–184.

6. Sweller, John. Cognitive Load Theory. Springer, 2011.

"Be regular and orderly in your life, so that you may be violent and original in your work."

– Gustave Flaubert, letter to Gertrude Tennant (1876)

INSIGHT STUDIO

A Mandala Journal

mandalaearth.com

Creative Director Ashley Quackenbush

MANUFACTURED IN CHINA

10 9 8 7 6 5 4 3 2 1